MW01679328

THE WILLOW MAIDEN

by Meghan Collins · pictures by Laszlo Gal

METHUEN CHILDREN'S BOOKS

Also illustrated by the award winning Laszlo Gal

The Twelve Dancing Princesses

The Little Mermaid

First Published in Great Britain 1986 by Methuen Children's Books Ltd
11 New Fetter Lane, London EC4P 4EE

Originally published in the United States by
Dial Books for Young Readers
A Division of E. P. Dutton
A Division of New American Library
Published in Great Britain 1986
Text copyright © 1985 by Meghan Collins
Illustrations copyright © 1985 by Laszlo Gal
Design by Atha Tehon
Printed in Hong Kong by South China Printing Co.
First edition
ISBN 0 416 48940 0

The full-color artwork was prepared using watercolor washes, gouache,
and colored pencils. It was then camera-separated and reproduced
as red, blue, yellow, and black halftones.

For Jack

M.C.

To all my friends at CBLFT News

L.G.

Late one night, a young farmer was riding alone down a country road beside a dark wood. He was going home from a fair in town, where there had been fireworks to celebrate Midsummer Night's Eve.

As he rode along, he noticed fat thunderclouds blowing in from the west. He quickened his horse's pace but was still many miles from his farm when he felt the first chilly raindrops on his shoulders.

Deciding it would be safer to take shelter, he turned his horse into the wood. To his surprise it balked after a few steps and stood shivering and flicking its ears.

"What's the matter, boy?" Denis asked, smoothing the horse's wet neck. "Oh, I know. We are in the Whispering Woods, aren't we? Well, calm down. We must stay here until the rain stops."

He dismounted, tied his horse to a tree, and settled himself on some dry leaves under a nearby rock ledge. Sitting there, he remembered the tales he had heard since childhood of the Whispering Woods.

Strong men — hunters and fishermen — who had got lost there after dark on a summer night, came out pale and shaking to tell of having been tormented with voices whispering around them, "Come this way, come this way." And every few years some young man would disappear altogether, never to be heard from again.

Now Denis shivered too. But he was always one to think he could take care of anything that happened with no help from anyone.

"After all," he reasoned, "if I hear whispers, I don't have to go."

Tired from his long day in town, Denis soon fell sound asleep.

When Denis woke after an hour or so, the rain had stopped. Hearing sounds, he thought at first it must be the night wind in the trees. But the closer he listened, the more it seemed like voices laughing and talking over a thin thread of music. Although good sense told him to ride away as fast as he could, curiosity was stronger.

He groped his way through the darkness toward the sounds, till he reached the edge of a clearing. So remarkable was the sight that met him, he could only stand and stare.

The clearing was beside a little lake that glittered under the moon. In the center a group of handsome people all dressed in green were seated at a long table that was set with a magnificent feast. At the head sat a man who must have been their king, for his chair was like a throne, and he wore a crown of green gold upon his head. Behind him a harpist and two fiddlers played gentle tunes.

Catching sight of Denis, a young woman rose from her place beside the king and walked toward him. She was slender in her dress of gauzy green; her long straight hair shone silver in the moonlight, and her face was one Denis thought he had been dreaming about all his life.

"Welcome," she said in a voice of chimes. "Won't you join us?"

She held out her hand, and because her smile was true, he followed.

"Who are you?" asked Denis. "I thought I knew everyone in the county."

"We are the Willow people," she replied. "My name is Lisane. Come, meet my father, the Willow King."

The king graciously invited Denis to sit between him and his daughter. They set a gold plate and a crystal cup before him and urged him to help himself.

Ah, here it is, thought Denis. This must be enchanted food, and after one bite of it, I shall probably turn into a toad.

"Is this safe for me to eat?" he asked Lisane in a low voice.

"Of course."

Denis decided that if he couldn't trust those clear green eyes, he couldn't trust anything in life, so he took a swallow from his cup and a taste of the fruit — the most delicious wine and the sweetest peach he had ever had. To his relief nothing happened, except that where he had taken the peach from the platter, another appeared in its place, and he saw that the wine flagon was just as full as it had been before his cup was poured.

When the guests had finished eating, the king clapped his hands and the musicians struck up a merry tune.

"Now there will be dancing," said Lisane, and she drew Denis to his feet. Looking over his shoulder as she led him away, he saw that the table with all its dishes and food was fading into a mist. In the time it took him to blink in disbelief, it was gone.

Denis and Lisane danced as if they were floating all alone in the clearing. Sometimes she whirled away from him, but they always drew back together. The other dancers began to turn to watch them, and from his throne the king followed their movements with an uneasy frown.

Denis noticed that Lisane's face was no longer so sparkling and lighthearted as it had been. When the music paused, she took his arm and walked a little apart from the others.

"You are in terrible danger," she whispered. "When strangers find us at our Midsummer Night's feast, we always make them welcome. But after the dancing, someone will suggest that we swim in the lake to cool off. One of our men will challenge you to a game, to see who can stay underwater the longer. You will never win. He will grab you and hold you under until you drown."

"I'd like to see him try! I am bigger and stronger than any man here."

"Oh, please believe me. It has happened to all who have found us. Don't you talk in your town of men who have come into the Whispering Woods and never been seen again?"

Denis's face told her he believed in the danger at last.

"I am going to leave for a short while, to bring something that will protect you. Do not for any reason go into the water until I come back."

"Lisane," he asked as she turned away, "why are you doing this for me, when not for the others?"

"Because," she murmured, so low he could scarcely hear, "because I love you."

Before he could answer, she was gone.

The music stopped, and from the gathering someone called, "Let us go swim!"

"Will you join them?" invited the Willow King. "The water will be cool after so much dancing."

"I will," said Denis, "but not yet."

"Where is Lisane?" grumbled the Willow King. "Perhaps she can persuade you."

Just then, Lisane came running from the forest. "Are you going swimming? Good!" she called loudly so the others could hear. Drawing close, she took his hand, and Denis felt something cold being pressed into his palm.

"It is a jar of oil from wild ducks," she whispered. "Rub it all over yourself, and no one will be able to hold you. Your skin will be so oily that you can slip away."

Denis nodded and closed his fist around the little jar. He stepped behind a tree to shed his clothes, rubbed the oil on himself, then went to join the others in the water.

The air was warm as new milk, and the moon spilled its light everywhere. Standing waist-deep in the water, the tallest and strongest of the Willow men hailed Denis with a friendly grin.

"My name is Jero," he said. "We thought you might like to try a game we sometimes play."

As Jero explained the rules, Denis remembered the men who had been drowned and felt a chill of fear.

" . . . and the one who can hold his breath the longer wins," concluded Jero. "Ready, friend?"

"Readier than you think, *friend*."

They waded farther out and turned to face each other. Denis saw Jero looking at him with a bright, pitiless stare like a fox.

At the same moment the two men took deep breaths and plunged underwater. When Jero came for him, Denis just had time to grasp Jero's upper arms as his own were being seized. Even forewarned, he was surprised by the Willow man's strength.

Denis tried to pit his muscle against Jero's, but try as he would, he could not free himself from that deadly grip. He struggled and struggled until he felt himself getting weak. Pain tightened like a strong belt around his chest. He knew he would soon have to breathe or die.

With all his willpower Denis forced himself to release Jero. Then he began to slide his arms free, slipping through Jero's hands. The Willow man squeezed tighter, but when Denis kept sliding, Jero let go and tried to catch Denis by the legs. It was no use. The oil from the wild ducks made Denis's skin so slippery, it was like trying to catch a trout with bare hands.

The instant Denis pulled his arms loose, he caught Jero by the hair, pushing him down to keep the Willow man from grabbing him again. Denis kicked

and pushed until his strength gave out, then let go. When he knew Jero had risen to the surface for breath, he, too, came up, gasping, a split second later.

There was silence from the shore, a long pause. Then the Willow people began to applaud and cheer for Denis. The two men waded ashore. Jero came toward Denis to shake his hand.

"No thanks, *friend,*" said Denis. "That last handshake you gave me was quite enough."

When Denis was dressed, the Willow King came to greet him.

"You are a strong man, or a lucky one. From now on, you shall be safe among my people, and if there is any favor you wish to ask me, I will grant it."

"I wish to marry your daughter, Lisane," said Denis, "if she will have me."

The king drew back, frowning. "That is impossible. Lisane is a Willow maiden."

Lisane stepped forward. "Father," she said, "I cannot be happy unless I am with Denis. Please."

The king gave a cry of pain and began to stride around.

"Young man," he warned, "we Willow people live inside our trees all year long except on Midsummer Night's Eve and the night of the harvest moon, when we come out to feast and dance. There is only one way a Willow maiden like Lisane can marry a mortal man. She can stay with you in the autumn and winter when her tree is sleeping, but she must return to it every spring — without fail. Can you agree to that?"

"Yes, indeed." Denis was willing to agree to anything, if only he could have Lisane for his wife.

"Then so be it," the king pronounced sadly. "Denis, you must leave Lisane here for the rest of the summer. If you are of the same mind, come back in the autumn. I promise you may be wed on the night of the harvest moon."

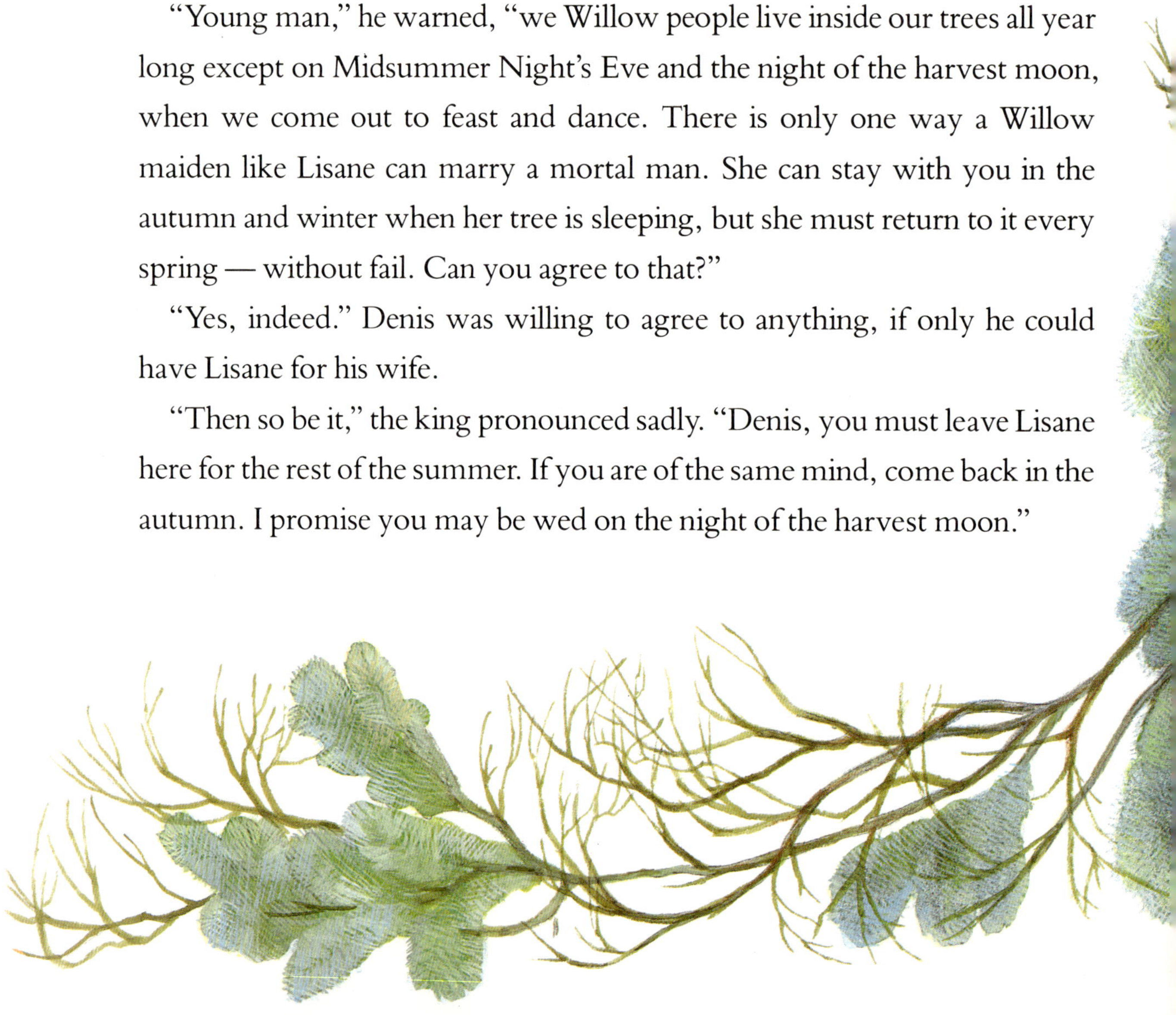

Lisane walked a little way into the woods with Denis to say good-bye.

"Before I go . . . which is your tree?" he asked.

"It is the willow by the big rock, near the water."

"I will come here often to visit while I am waiting for you. Will you know when I am near?"

"Yes, I will know."

They twined together in a farewell kiss, and their parting was for each of them like a tearing of roots.

That summer seemed to Denis the longest of his life. He labored so hard to prepare his farmhouse for Lisane that each night he fell on his bed like a stone and was asleep in three breaths. Every week he rode to the Whispering Woods and walked to where Lisane's tree stood by the lake. He sat in her shade and tossed pebbles into the water while he told her what he had been doing since he was last there. Each time, she let one little jade-green leaf fall into his hand to let him know she heard.

At last the new moon of September appeared in the west. Slow as apples growing, it got larger and larger until finally the night of the full harvest

moon came. Denis dressed with care in the new clothes he had bought, and put in his pocket the heavy gold wedding ring that had once belonged to his mother.

On the ride to the Whispering Woods his thoughts seesawed between joy and dread. First he imagined Lisane coming to him, beautiful beyond telling in her wedding dress. Next he pictured the forest black and still with no one there to greet him, all his hopes gone. Perhaps Midsummer Night's Eve had never really happened, but was just a spell cast over him by the magic of the Whispering Woods.

When he reached the lake, however, the scene that met his eyes was all he had ever wished. The Willow King was sitting on his throne, the magic table was set for a wedding supper, and there among the men and maidens was Lisane, wearing a gown and misty veil of softest yellow gold.

Lisane and Denis knelt while an Oak-tree bishop led them through their marriage vows. The king gave his blessing, and the Willow people circled round them, carrying lighted candles.

After the wedding feast there was dancing until dawn, and when Denis was ready to take his bride home, the only sad face to be seen was that of the Willow King.

"Don't be downhearted, Father," said Lisane, hugging him in farewell. "I will be back in the spring."

The old king shook his head. "Promises are easy to make."

So Lisane rode off, sitting in front of Denis, with her golden gown fluttering.

At home Denis carried Lisane across the threshold, and she walked slowly through the rooms, for she had never been in a house before.

"What's that?" she asked, pointing to the fireplace and the broom and the bed, and she laughed aloud to hear the mantel clock strike the hour.

That winter was a time of discovery for each of them. For Denis, even though he had lived in the country all his life, the surprise was the world of nature. Lisane taught him the ways of birds and plants and weather as Denis had never known them before. She could tell by the touch of air on her skin

when it would freeze or thaw, and she could hear a badger in his lair at the roots of a tree.

And Lisane had to learn the daily life of human beings, for there was no magic table here to bring whatever she wanted.

The only thing that made Denis unhappy was the rush of time. When, after the New Year, Lisane remarked upon how quickly the days grew longer, he made a joke to change the subject. Yet it was impossible to stop the change of seasons.

Lisane showed him a jack-in-the-pulpit she found by the brook. Snowdrops bloomed. Then one night came the sound Denis had been dreading — the first rising chorus of spring peepers down by the pond, an unmistakable sign that winter was past.

Denis's good nature left him. "Why can you only be here in winter?" he asked.

"Because I must go back to my tree in spring or it will die."

Denis fell silent, but in his heart the feeling grew ever stronger. He could not bear to have her leave him.

One day, Lisane said she absolutely must go before the week was out. Lying awake that night, Denis had the idea that he knew would solve their troubles.

Should he tell Lisane? he wondered. No, he would not say a word. His plan was so daring that he wanted to rush ahead before he lost his nerve.

Next morning he told Lisane that he was going to town to buy seed. She wanted to go too, but he said the sack of seed would be all the weight his horse could carry home. Her pure green eyes looked into his, and Denis felt uneasy, as if she could read his thoughts.

"Dearest, you must learn to let me go free when I need to," she said. "I will always come back to you."

On the ride to the Whispering Woods, Denis would not let himself think of what he was about to do. He reached the familiar clearing, and saw the gnarled old king willow-tree, but turned his head as if avoiding someone's eyes.

There at the edge of the lake stood Lisane's tree. Denis grabbed the axe he had brought in his saddlebag and raised it. But just as he was gathering all his strength to swing, a sudden thought stopped him. His heart began to pound with terror. What was he doing?

Furious at himself, he flung the axe far out over the lake. It wheeled through the air and fell into the water with a heavy splash. Then, weakened from fear at what he had nearly done, he sat down on a rock beside the tree and bowed his head to his knees.

As he crouched there motionless, he thought about what had almost happened, how blind he had been not to realize that by cutting down her tree, he might have killed Lisane as well. A slender branch from her tree, swaying in the wind, brushed the back of his neck. He glanced upward, caught the branch in his hand and studied it more closely. The tip was dry and brown.

For the first time since he had arrived, Denis looked around the clearing. The other willows that surrounded him were all flecked with bright new leaves on green branches, yet Lisane's tree still hung down in bare golden chains that were beginning to wither. And suddenly, Denis's sadness and confusion fell away. He knew what he must do, no matter how hard it might be.

As fast as he could, Denis ran back to the road where he had left his horse, untied it, and swung into the saddle.

"Come on, boy, there's no time to lose," he said. "We've got to bring her back home."